Learning out of school

K.A.

TOKE.

Learning out of school

A teachers' guide to the educational use of museums

Molly Harrison

Ward Lock Educational

0 7062 3051 5 ✓
First published 1954
Completely revised and reset 1970

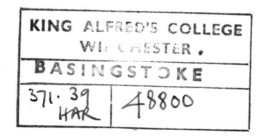
Set in 11 on 12 point Plantin
Printed by Butler & Tanner Limited, Frome and London
for Ward Lock Educational Limited
116 Baker Street, London W1M 2BB
Made in England

Contents

Dedication

With affection I dedicate this book to the many colleagues who have shared with me, during thirty years, the enjoyment and challenge of working in the Geffrye Museum. It has always been as a team, sharing common ideals and purposes, that we have talked and worked, argued and laughed together. And this book, too, is in the same pattern. It is a result of many hours of talk, of many people's thoughts, experience, disappointments and achievements. I know they all share my hope that it may be a service to teachers and thus an enrichment to children, in their learning and their living.

27th September 1969

Acknowledgments

The author and publishers would like to thank the following for their help in providing the photographs which illustrate this book: Colchester Museum photograph facing page 16; Fox Photos photographs facing pages 17 and 32; L & M Taylor Limited photographs facing page 33; Kidbrooke Park Junior School photograph facing page 48; Geffrye Museum photographs facing pages 49 and 65; Rowledge Primary School photograph facing page 64; also the Comptroller of Her Majesty's Stationery Office for permission to reproduce material which appears as appendix three.

to know
Rather consists in opening out a way
Whence the imprisoned splendour may escape
Than in effecting entry for a light
Supposed to be without.

Robert Browning *Paracelsus*

Introduction

W hy?

Education everywhere is on the move and in this country more than any other. In spite of economic pressures changes are taking place and all our children now have fuller opportunities than those available to any previous generation.

Many of the changes stem from progressive views of what education is about and five of them in particular are related to the idea that learning can take place out of school as well as in school.

Firstly there is a growing concern to widen children's horizons. The cloister idea of education is out and more and more people realize that a child is more likely to learn to live creatively in the world if he has not been separated from that world while he is growing up. This does not of course detract from the great importance of education *in* school but underlines the idea that education at home, in the club, the street, the theatre, the museum and the library is just as fruitful and that parents and teachers need to consider the child's environment as a whole.

Secondly there is a growing concern that teaching should relate to the individual and to the late twentieth century. All our knowledge is gained through personal experience and nothing can be really understood unless it is put, to some extent, into that context.

Thirdly there is a growing realization that learning is an active process for the young and not a mere passive listening. We all learn more in life by imitation, by infection and from experience than we do by instruction.

Fourthly there is a growing concern that teaching should no longer be treated in watertight compartments. Breaking down interdisciplinary barriers, team teaching, the integrated day—these are among the most hopeful of today's educational trends. It makes obvious sense to help the young mind to jump barriers between subjects, as between classes, nationalities and races.

Fifthly there is growing concern that education should help young people to cope with an age of increased leisure. It makes

9

obvious sense to foster out of school interests so that the momentum of interest may continue when compulsory schooling finishes.

These five trends are not new; they are changes of emphasis and priority which amount almost to a change of scene. It is because the scene has altered considerably in the last fifteen years that a new and enlarged edition of this book is being issued. The viewpoint expressed is very much as it was, but the text now includes a wider concept of learning. Some of the arguments, too, are different because the sixties and seventies are very different from the forties and fifties.

Taking a group of lively young people out of school is still not easy; in fact in some ways it becomes more difficult as new horizons, new methods and a better diet make lively youngsters livelier. It is certainly not a rest or a morning off for the teacher. There are many practical difficulties, problems which are general as well as others which are particular. There are many opportunities which can very easily be missed, methods which can fail to strike home, sparks of real interest which may not light, all for want of careful planning.

This book is written with these problems in mind in the hope that more teachers and more parents too may be encouraged to explore their neighbourhood with their children as a beginning to new interests, activities and ideas.

Chapter one

Why take children out?

Why indeed—is the journey really necessary? There are parents and teachers who have their doubts about this; 'The function of the school is to teach the children' they say 'and there is already too little time to get through all that has to be done'.

This point of view is understandable even if one disagrees with it. All new trends in education seem to require more time, yet the school day and the school week remain the same. Citizenship is now thought of as essential for the older children. French starts earlier and earlier with the juniors, domestic economy classes need more time than mere cookery did, crafts demand a liberal slice of the week and activities have to be fitted in for all subjects. Indeed, the very concept of a formal timetable divided into subjects is rapidly disappearing and the children's interests give the main impetus to the work in more and more schools. The only commodity which does not change is time.

Are school visits to museums worth while, with hours so precious and so many practical problems involved? Aren't the children better off in the classroom? There are changing fashions in education as in everything else and opinion is now swinging towards a wider view of learning than was previously accepted. We no longer think that learning happens only at a set time, in a special place put aside for the purpose, when somebody decides to talk about a specific subject. It can and often does happen at unexpected times—in the bathroom, in a bus, in front of the television screen or at the cinema and certainly in even the least promising art gallery or museum.

What can boys and girls gain from a museum visit? This depends of course upon the exhibits and upon the arrangement and atmosphere of the museum, but all exhibits can, in varying degrees, give evidence and a sense of reality. They can fire the imagination; they can set standards and widen horizons; they can help to develop the ability to concentrate, explore and observe;

II

above all they can be enjoyed. Let us look more closely at these very varied potentials.

Evidence and reality

Seeing is believing and teachers and parents know that something fundamental comes alive in any child when he can see, touch and handle. Museums contain real things, things that have been made or used or collected by people for some special reason. Although classroom work is becoming more and more practical, there are of course limits to the seeing, handling and doing that are possible there, so a visit to see the real things follows naturally from many a lesson. Practical experience can enter where theory reigned before. The value of the museum visit lies not so much in new facts discovered as in the reality and life given to familiar facts.

If we want our children to learn to think for themselves we must give them plenty of opportunity of finding things out, of questioning accepted beliefs and checking wherever checking is possible. We must ask them and we must expect them to ask us from time to time how we know this, that or the other, where this originated, how the author and the illustrator know. And if we do talk and question in this way in the classroom it may surprise us how often we will have to go, not only to the library, but to the museum and to the museum publications.

Imagination

However it is not the prime purpose of a museum to pass on facts. Facts there are in plenty in any museum and if the exhibits are well and pleasingly displayed then the facts will gain enormously by their visual presentation. The museum exhibit, the painting or piece of sculpture in an art gallery have in addition other non material values in which we can share once we become aware of them. They can help us respond to peoples, places and situations far removed from ourselves. These words of Bertrand Russell's underline one of the great responsibilities facing all those who deal with young people: *We know too much and feel too little. At least, we feel too little of those creative emotions from which a good life springs. In regard to what is important we are passive, where we are active it is over trivialities.*

The museum or art gallery can help us to see something 'from which a good life springs' and they can, in a sense, do something to restore a balance to the way we bring up our children. There is magic there even when the display is less than good, and sometimes just because the display is indifferent and unlike the sophistication of the world outside. And magic is an ingredient which the modern child too often misses. In a flat, or in a city street, there can be no 'fairies at the bottom of the garden', there is little wonder or delight which cannot be explained away, for our matter of fact ways of thinking and living do not even stress the wonders which do exist, The magic of the electric light, the telephone, the aeroplane, the television—these and much more become accepted fairly soon.

But a child who has no fairies in the garden can perhaps find them in his museum. He can wander among strange and unfamiliar things and picture something of the life of those who use and make them: he can see things remote in time or obscure in purpose and enjoy them quite apart from their intellectual interest; he can thrill to the colours of a bird's wing or a fish's scales, to the craftsmanship of a fine pot or piece of glass, to the intricacy and power of a vast machine. All these can evoke a powerful response in the child and by appealing directly to his feelings inspire him to the degree to which they caught his imagination.

Setting standards

Contact with good things, things which are outstanding in their field, can train our eyes to a remarkable degree and museums and galleries usually do contain things of outstanding visual quality. Just to look at them can set standards providing some interpretation is given. If we take boys and girls to look at fine things and discuss their workmanship, their uses and their durability, we shall be giving them a standard which they can refer to whenever they have practical choices to make. If we show them a lovely Greek vase we can point out its texture, its proportion, its age, its rarity and the quality of its decoration and the class may well be impressed and awed. If on the other hand we discuss how it was made and point out that it was used to store olive oil and later compare it with sauce bottles and jars used at home, we are sharpening their eyes and making them critical of the everyday things they use and buy. Until more people are critical we cannot hope to live in more inviting and attractive towns and villages, homes or schools.

Widening horizons

It is sometimes astonishing to see how small a child's world can be. From home to school, from school to home, to grandma's on Saturday and to auntie's on Sunday—for many children that is all they know of their community and therefore all they appear to want to know. They may, through television and the cinema, be relatively familiar with foreign countries but know little of immediate realities. But once taken out of school—not home or to grandma's or aunty's, but on a new bus route or to a different station see how their eyes light up and the questions bubble. Travelling, seeing new places, coming into contact with different sorts of people and things can be an education in itself and confidence grows with each occasion. Confidence not only in oneself but in the response of those around—the helpfulness of the bus conductor, the advice given by a fellow passenger, or the friendly joke from a policeman—all these are people of whom many children have to *learn* not to be afraid or shy. They will learn a great deal from watching an adult deal in a friendly calm way with the difficulties encountered on a journey. We need to remember that we are on stage all the time and that by our actions we teach a great deal about social behaviour as well as about ourselves.

Learning to live in one's community is one of the most difficult aspects of growing up. Learning to move about freely within it, to ask for help in a friendly manner and therefore to receive it, to dress and behave in ways that are individual without attracting unnecessary attention, to learn gradually what there is to do and see and know and enjoy are vital skills which children must acquire if they are to gain maximum benefit from their environment.

Boredom or enjoyment

There is something quite incredible in the extent to which people today seem to be bored. This creeping paralysis is constantly growing for many boys' or girls' creative abilities that might have enriched their leisure hours wither through lack of use and lack of practice and sparks that once glowed are so easily stifled by the humdrum, unfulfilling interests of pay packet and mass entertainment. Leisure is indeed a problem for us all; either we have far too little of it and cannot ever hope to do all the absorbing things we long to, or we seem to have more time than we know how to use up and so let it run to waste.

Any excursion out of the classroom that can help children to know what there is to do, what interests there are to follow up in their district, is a valuable preparation for after school leisure. An early taste for museum visiting may lead to hobbies and interests which can do much to enliven and enrich adult years and help to counteract some of the more negative aspects of our modern society. Out of school visits and classroom teaching can only hope to sow the seeds of interests—the flowering can only come from a lifelong cultivation. One boy or girl who discovers today that a museum visit can be fun means tomorrow an adult or a young family whose leisure hours will be all the richer and more truly fulfilling.

Chapter two

How do we take them out?

It really is essential to know beforehand what you are going to see and why. Hearsay, hope or faith are no substitute for a solid purpose and at least three quarters of the value of any visit will be lost if it is not well prepared.

Organize it yourself

It should go without saying that arrangements must be made beforehand, but what does need saying is that the arrangements for your class must be made by you yourself. In these days of larger and larger schools, there is a growing tendency for the practical details of a proposed visit to be left to the school secretary and this can cause great difficulty. However efficient the secretary may be, he or she cannot be expected to know exactly what your plans for your children are. Bare facts about date, time and place can be settled by another person so long as there are no queries to be answered and no alternatives to be discussed. But good planning involves far more than bare facts. This is not a matter of not trusting a colleague, but of having confidence in your own purposes and your own skill in carrying them out and of knowing that another's view is sure to differ from your own.

Much worse confusion is caused if a visit is not arranged beforehand at all. Even large museums and art galleries where space is normally no problem find it helpful to know that you propose to bring a party of children, for they may have planned some special function on that day or for a variety of other reasons they may prefer you to delay your visit until another time. This is a matter of courtesy but in dealing with a small museum far more than courtesy is necessary. In the case of smaller buildings of any kind it is essential for them to be able to space their group visitors and to arrange a programme accordingly. If you arrive without prior notice you may be turned away or have to confine your group to a section of the museum they did not want to see.

2. Cava

whic

This girl may never have known a civil war, but wearing a Cromwellian helmet can help her imagine some of the anxieties of that time.

A life size seventeenth century gentleman, made of wire and dressed in paper, stands solidly alongside appliqué paper chairs of the period with a stencilled tapestry behind.

Few words need be wasted on the group which arrives un-heralded and whose teacher replies to a tactful question with 'we usually go swimming on Tuesday afternoons but the baths are closed today' or 'the history mistress is off sick this week and the head told us to take this class to the nearest museum'. It is not unknown for this to happen and it is surely no coincidence that children brought in this way are usually undisciplined and looking for trouble.

Arranging with the museum — *INTERNET*

It is very important for the teacher who is to take the class out to visit the museum beforehand; in fact only if you have seen what the museum has to offer can you possibly know whether a visit will be right for your children or not. Not only must you know what there is to *see* but you must have discussions with the museum staff, find out where the lavatories are, know your route thoroughly and be able to interest the children in whatever they can see on the way. There is far more educational value in an out of school visit than just the specific place you have arranged to go and see.

A preliminary visit must be paid some time before the date of a group visit if anything of value is to be passed on to the children and to avoid muddles in the organization of the many practical details which can do so much to make or mar an outing for youngsters. If you want them to feel welcome and if you want them to be catered for in whatever ways are possible, you must make sure that their visit is expected. You should write initially to the director of the museum, unless you are certain that the chief officer is called the curator as is usually the case in a small museum.

The museum staff can only do a really good job if they get the fullest cooperation from the school. If they are suddenly presented with a group of young people about whom they know nothing, it is a little optimistic to expect them to strike just the right note. Each group is different from all the others, particularly in this country where individual schools are allowed an enormous amount of freedom in which to develop those educational methods which the teachers feel are best. No one class's requirements will be just like another's.

What must the museum teacher or lecturer or keeper know

about your children if the visit you arrange is to be successful? He or she must of course know how many children are coming and must have agreed that the museum can take that number; their age and type must be known too as this will determine who will deal with them. It is also important to know the special line of interest, syllabus, project or subject that they have been following at school.

In addition it will be helpful if the museum staff can be given an idea of the type of teaching which the children are accustomed to. For instance are they used to working largely on their own and able to use reference material freely or do they normally expect to sit and listen to their teacher in relative silence? Do they ask questions readily? Are they accustomed to drawing? Do they normally work individually or in small groups, or will they feel lost unless they are all doing the same piece of work? Are they of average or mixed ability? Do they have special language difficulties or physical or mental handicaps and so on? All these facts will inevitably affect the attitude and the behaviour of the children and allowances have to be made for them. A good museum teacher will deal differently with every group.

It is most important that the class teacher does not give any of this information to the museum staff in front of the children and it is very sad that this common courtesy is not always observed. Some apparently civilized adults who would not dream of commenting in public about a friend or passing a remark about an acquaintance, will sometimes forget themselves sufficiently to say when they bring a group of boys and girls into a museum: 'These are not very bright', 'these are D stream', 'you will find these won't listen for long' or some other similarly insulting remark. This is probably not rudely meant but it is thoughtless, it is unkind and it will very effectively lower the children's opinion of themselves and of their potential when these are already perilously low. Building up is surely more helpful than knocking down and we all tend to behave very much as we are expected to.

A specialist in any particular subject is not necessarily able to help young people understand and enjoy specialist material and there is growing agreement in museums that those who are to work with children need some special kind of experience or training. Many museums now have on their staffs one or more trained and experienced teachers who have special knowledge of the museum's exhibits and are well able to interest boys and girls in them. They probably know the dangers of talking too much for too long and in difficult language; they certainly know how to manage a group well and how to draw a response from the most silent child as well as from the talkative ones. You can safely make your arrangements with them but it is important to remember that the museum is physically cut off from school life and that the museum staff are therefore working in the dark if they do not know what the class teacher is planning and what the children want to do.

Arranging with your head

It is not easy, from the point of view of school organization, for boys and girls to be taken out to visit places of interest and it is understandable that some head teachers are still dubious whether any value gained can offset the disruption of the timetable. Inevitably a visit will require more time than is usually given to the particular subject involved, inevitably there will be more children in the class than can conveniently travel in a group, there may be staff away at the last moment, or an important visitor may call and delay arrangements. There are a hundred and one contingencies that busy heads can foresee as likely to cause difficulty, but nevertheless the idea that educational visits are an important and essential part of education is gaining ground all the time.

But what if your particular head is less progressive or so burdened with administrative problems that he will not allow you to take your children out? Should you give in, miss the opportunity and deny your children the enjoyment?

Try to get your head to visit the museum and see what it has to offer but if persuasion fails you must try example. Take the group after school or on Saturday, make sure that every detail is so well planned, every activity so interesting, that the children will do the persuading for you. They will return home and to school so full of the interest and the fun of the excursion, the drawings and models and charts and writings which they produce will be so lively, that it will be obvious to everyone—including your head—that you know how to conduct a really good visit so that it is education in the fullest sense.

Arranging for a coach

Of course it is best for your children if you take them about on public transport for this is an education in itself, but as buses and trains become increasingly crowded more school groups are taken out by coach. As more visits are arranged, coach companies become more demanding and more autocratic, until the absurd point is reached when the length of a visit has to be determined by the convenience of the coach company or the driver!

A vehicle is a convenience for which a customer pays accepted rates; he has, therefore, the right to state his wishes and to expect that they will be met. Traffic congestion can make difficulties but if for any other reason your coach cannot start or finish the journey at the time you want, you should write to the managing director and complain. If your wishes are still not met you should go to another company. If they form a ring and you cannot get satisfaction from any of them, it is time to begin to think whether the school should not have its own bus.

Some schools raise money for this purpose by jumble sales, fêtes and peformances and when they have a bus of their own they find many unexpected uses for it. But if teachers would be firmer with the bus driver and not put up with conditions which militate against the children's best interests, the companies would probably be far more cooperative.

Preparing the children

There is unlikely to be any opposition from the children themselves to the idea of going out. Much as they may enjoy their daily school life, they will yet welcome almost any opportunity to see something fresh, to explore the world outside, to meet other people and do different things. This enthusiasm is of course a great contribution toward the success of any visit and the wise teacher will be ready to build upon it.

There is always a danger, however, that the children may think of their visit as just an outing and that they may be so over-excited that they miss the essence of the whole exercise. It is important for them to be in a fully receptive and appreciative state of mind, knowing where they are going and why, and with a clear idea of what they are going to aim at during their visit and in their work afterwards. All this will develop naturally if the teacher who is responsible for the visit plans intelligently and well. An unprepared, unplanned visit to even the most important and interesting exhibition is of no more value than an excursion to the circus; indeed the circus is more obviously fun and so far more valuable.

How much preparation should you give them? This will of course depend upon your purpose and upon the children's experience and ability. It would be a pity to do in class whatever you are taking them to the museum to see, but it would be worse not to bring them to the point of maximum interest. Skill is needed here, so that appetites are whetted and no more; foresight is needed so that even the journey itself is enjoyable and there are things to look for en route; discipline is needed so that your group behave in a reasonable way and are therefore acceptable at the museum. Nothing spoils a visit more for everyone concerned than noisy, untidy, selfish behaviour on the part of a group. You must remember—and so must they—that they are on show in more senses than one. They are ambassadors and if for any reason they behave badly attitudes will harden towards the next school group who visit that particular museum.

Arrangements with parents

Only rarely will parents have any objection to their son or daughter going on an educational visit. Most people nowadays realize the value and the significance of widening a child's horizons and enlarging his experience. But you may receive a note informing you that 'my Johnnie gets sick on a bus' or 'our Mary has bad legs' and this you will have to investigate. Of course you know already—and you check regularly—the health and spirits and worries of your children, so the refusing note will be in a certain context. Perhaps Johnny's mother does not know that there are several types of tranquillizing drugs that can completely prevent travel sickness if the right type is taken—so you can find an opportunity of telling her this. Perhaps Jane's headache will respond to aspirin, or perhaps it has a deeper non physical cause and stems from fear, or from mother's wish that her daughter should be at home to look after the baby. Your knowledge of the individual child and contact with the parents will, in time, help you to sort out the simpler causes from the deeper ones and act accordingly. Mothers need to know in good time if you want the children to take a sandwich lunch; there may be some special requirement in clothing or equipment and perhaps you plan to leave school early or to get back late. On all these matters a duplicated note to mother is more reliable than a message.

How many will you take out?
An honest answer would be as few as possible, for it is obvious that a small group can see better, hear better, move about more easily and discuss things more sensibly than a large group can.

However this obvious truth is no help to teachers who have to cope with forty children in a class. It may seem impossible to subdivide a class in order to take out half at a time, but that should certainly be aimed at. If the relationships within the school are friendly you will be able to swap responsibility with another member of staff now and then.

You will probably want to have another adult with you and if you are taking twenty children or more you will have to by LEA statute. Who will you take? The decision may not be yours but you may well have a say. The temptation will be to ask a friend to go with you or a colleague who shares your interest, but it is worth considering whether this is really in the best interests of the children. If a colleague of an entirely different speciality and subject goes with you, you will have the challenge and interest of seeing the material and judging the experience from another point of view and the children will be helped to see and enjoy all the more. There will be two extra pairs of eyes to help them and not only one.

Your view on this point will be coloured by the overall purpose in your teaching and your particular purpose in arranging the museum visit. If you are mainly concerned that the children should learn what they are told about the exhibits, then it is probably best if both adults taking them accept the same views. If you want to help them to think, to question and evaluate evidence, then it will obviously be of great help to them if they can see that opinions differ.

Throughout life everyone has to thread their way through conflicting statements and differing points of view. There are very few matters upon which experts do not differ as much as amateurs and it is surely wise to let this fact become a part of children's learning—both in school as well as out of school. So if an art teacher goes to see historical material with a history teacher, a craft teacher looks at geographical material with a geographer and an English specialist goes with anybody, everyone's experience will have been enriched and their eyes and minds sharpened. More and more groups visiting museums are accompanied by parents as well as teachers. This is splendid and can do nothing but good so long as it is the teacher who is finally in charge.

Whoever goes, do keep the numbers down and resist the pressures of those who have to think only in terms of value for money. From an economic point of view it is wrong to send fewer children than a bus or a train can carry; from an educational point of view it will most certainly be wrong to send so many children that their visit loses most of its value.

Some museums make no stipulations about numbers in a group, but most doubt seriously the value of large groups. Some do state their limitations and these may well differ for different ages, and therefore different sizes, of children and for different rooms, galleries and exhibits. It is impossible to lay down hard and fast rules, but without a doubt the fewer the better. You *must* consult the museum of your choice.

How much to see?

The greatest danger that assails anyone visiting a museum, art gallery or country house is indigestion—mental, emotional, visual, physical indigestion which comes from trying to see too much. Not even the most voracious and most knowledgeable adult can hope to look at a collection of things for more than a limited time and really see and enjoy them. Eyes become dulled, feelings overstimulated and confused, mind muddled and feet aching. How much more is that true of children visiting a collection in a group —they start off full of enthusiasm, try to rush round if they are not checked and end up by seeing nothing at all, feeling tired and disgruntled and disliking anything connected with art.

It is absolutely essential to control the general course of their visit and equally essential that they shall not have the feeling that they are being taken round by someone who has a fixed idea of what they ought to see.

What a world of difference there is between looking round a museum and looking *for* something in one. The former has a passive flavour—starting with picture or object number one and following the catalogue through to the end. It suggests a sheep like acceptance of all that somebody has arranged and nearly always results in an unseeing stare. Looking for, on the other hand, implies keen search for specific things of interest and a lively discussion of them with friends.

For example, anyone who takes a group of children to look round the National Gallery is surely lacking in any understanding either of children or of paintings. But a group of relatively young, or relatively dull boys and girls can enjoy a visit to that same National Gallery to see, for instance, seventeenth century Dutch paintings so long as there is a purpose, be it historical, geographical, aesthetic, literary or a combination of all these, and their vision is not clouded by trying to look, on the same day, at paintings of another century or another country.

Yet the idea of looking round is by no means dead, either among museum people themselves or among visitors from schools or elsewhere. Sometimes a general tour of the gallery is asked for and normally, in one small museum at any rate, it is refused, reasons are given and an alternative is proposed. This alternative usually takes the form of a discussion on a specific theme or a specific period. In larger museums a group will often be offered a brief introductory talk followed by suggestions of things to do and things to look out for. Anything less than this is likely to be a waste of everybody's time.

It is a good idea for the museum teacher to have an introductory chat with the children if possible. It makes everyone feel at ease, takes the edge off the initial strangeness and sets a relaxed tone for the visit. It may draw attention to the building, if it is an historic one, or to the arrangements of the displays; it may warn against certain misunderstandings, give an idea of what the museum is trying to say and why, and can make all the difference between an aimless meandering visit and a purposeful, intelligent selection of what to see.

Avoid, if you possibly can, the set lecture. Modern boys and girls are becoming more accustomed in school to pursuing their own interests at their own pace and they may not welcome an hour spent listening to somebody unless the talk is extremely well done. Moreover the whole purpose of the visit is to look at worth-while things, not merely to hear about them.

The bigger the museum, the more difficult it is to take young people to see it and the more essential it is to concentrate attention upon certain aspects and to be very firm about the importance of sticking to those aspects. There are as many different ways of concentrating their attention as there are different exhibits, different children and different teachers. A duplicated plan of the building with arrows showing the parts that are to be visited this time, an outline of some kind, a brief very simple guide, these are but a few of the possible ways of reducing the complicated mass of interesting things that are gathered in a large collection to something nearer the dimensions that a child can understand and enjoy. It is a good idea to treat any large collection as being in fact a number of smaller ones and to deal with each separately.

Of course you will at some time or another allow for a certain amount of exploration. How much and when will depend entirely upon the purpose of your visit, whether it is one occasion or part of a series, how the museum is arranged and the age of your children. In a small museum, particularly if it has a definite theme, there may be good reason in allowing a bird's eye view for a short time if that is possible. In a large museum a bird's eye view is just so much nonsense and leads to nothing less than indigestion of mind and feelings and acute weariness of body. Nothing more than a few leading thoughts can be suggested here. Be guided at all times by the individual factors in your situation and always remind the children that there will be other opportunities of visiting and that if they are keen to see something in particular they can come back on their own or with family or friends on Saturday.

Museum teachers

There is much to be said for arranging for someone on the museum staff to deal with the group for at least a part of the visit. Even if this is not the normal arrangement it may well be worth while asking for a little help in this way. There is value in a different voice, a new personality and approach even when, as is sometimes the case, it might be inadvisable to ask for more than a few minutes' initial attention. Museum staff are very willing to be helpful in such matters if you make your needs known. They are often only too conscious of their inexperience in talking to children and have little or no knowledge of present day educational techniques but they can do a turn, as it were, to the advantage of everyone.

Of course the situation is entirely different in the rapidly increasing number of museums which employ one or more teachers on their staff. In these cases the temptation for the visiting teacher may be to withdraw too much from the situation and leave the lesson so completely to the museum staff that valuable opportunities for discussion are likely to be lost.

This was in no way typical but I myself can remember an occasion when a teacher accompanying a class went comfortably off to sleep during a lesson and our discussions were rudely interrupted in the middle of a warm afternoon by the snores of 'Sir' sitting at the back. This helped nobody, much as one sympathized perhaps with his exhaustion. Equally difficult to surmount is the clicking of needles when a busy teacher wishes to fill every minute and fails to sense that her knitting is a gross intrusion. On such an occasion one just has to point out that the jumper could perhaps wait until the evening.

Less dramatic but equally unethical are the occasions when accompanying teachers decide to go and have coffee while the children are looking, listening and discussing. Obviously a teacher who has dozed or read, or gone off for coffee or to look at other parts of the museum while his class was busy about the purpose of their visit, cannot hope to follow up that purpose intelligently and fully when they are all back in the classroom. Even more important, what is the child to think of exhibits which their teacher does not seem to find interesting, of a talk which appears to be less important than coffee or a discussion in which their teacher does not wish to join? However well the museum teacher may put across the exhibits, the class teacher, on this occasion at least, is saying very effectively that these are not really worth bothering about. If that is indeed so the visit should never have taken place; if it is not so it is a pity for any teacher to appear to despise them. We need to remember that our actions do indeed speak louder than our words.

Chapter three

When do we take them out?

Ideally a museum visit should arise spontaneously for each child, but in practice of course we have to take into account the needs of a group of children as well as a variety of other factors—when opportunity occurs, when there is time to arrange a visit, when the powers that be will allow it and so on. There are endless factors leading to a fully ripe moment and no amount of generalization could cover them all, but we must try as far as possible to choose the moment when the children themselves are ready. They need to be ready physically, mentally and emotionally.

Firstly, of course, we must be sure they are old enough to cope with the upset involved in taking them out. They must be able to stand a journey and a certain amount of walking round without becoming too excited and overtired. Most children at the junior stage still find everything exciting and their attention span is still comparatively short so unless you are fortunate enough to have a museum or art gallery virtually round the corner and can make repeated short visits it will probably be as well to postpone going until the children are at least nine years old.

In any case groups of any age travelling a distance need time in which to recover from their journey before going into the museum. This is particularly true when they are on an extended school journey, studying a particular neighbourhood in a concentrated way. The temptation then is very strong to overcrowd the time and attempt too much too quickly.

Modern pressures tend to make us want to force the pace for our youngsters. We forget sometimes that with luck they have a lifetime ahead of them. Everything, we feel, must be done now and we teach as if the boys and girls in our care would drop dead the moment schooling ends.

In any museum there is too much to see and do, there are always too many places for our children to visit and so we can never get round to them all but we need to make sure that this fact does not make us attempt too much too soon. Time to digest and time to enjoy what they are busy about in school may well, for most juniors, be more important than any outside stimulation.

It is important that children shall have had sufficient experience before their visit to be able to grasp the main outline of ideas presented in a museum. Those who cannot read fairly fluently, no matter what their age, will probably miss a good deal of the point in most museums unless particular care is taken in preparation. This does not imply that only the more intelligent academic type of child can appreciate a visit to a museum. This is a fairly widespread misconception that needs correcting; museum collections can, if well used, interest virtually anybody. The special problems relating to visits by the physically, mentally or socially handicapped are important and are dealt with in chapter seven.

Those who are fortunate enough to have a museum very close to their school can pay more spontaneous visits than those who have to travel a distance and often a seemingly spontaneous visit may be just what is wanted. Its spontaneity will be seeming only to the children, of course, for we have already discussed the overwhelming importance of arranging visits beforehand.

Spontaneity is possible when you have a museum nearby; examples of mimicry and of protective colouring in insects, birds and mammals can be seen in the local history collection within a very short time of their discussion or treatment in class; the local record office will probably yield interesting documents dealing with some current ceremonial just at the moment when the children's interest in the matter is at its height. Fortunate indeed is the teacher who is so situated, both geographically and in terms of friendly cooperation, that he or she can make use of such facilities exactly when they are most useful.

But most schools are not near enough to a museum, art gallery or record office for frequent, short, immediate visits of that kind to be possible. Normally much longer term planning is essential and some detailed arrangements have to be made beforehand. The teacher has to make a guess as to when will be the most suitable moment, from the children's point of view, to pay a visit.

Nowadays in a growing number of schools there is a tendency for the pace of the work and even its scope and direction to be determined by the children themselves and their interests and ability rather than by a rigid timetable or syllabus, so it is not easy for a teacher to guess which stage in their work a class will have reached by a certain time. The children may not keep up to schedule or may forge ahead faster than anyone imagined, but that is a risk that has to be taken and it is not a very great one. No great harm is done if a visit has to be postponed because the class are not ready for it, but postponed it ought to be if timing has gone awry and the planned date is premature. There is no sense at all in visiting St Paul's Cathedral if the children are still busy with Joan of Arc, or a gallery of Victorian paintings if they are studying the costumes of the protagonists in the Civil War!

Most officials would understand such a situation if it were explained to them and would try sympathetically to fit in the visit later on. The one cardinal sin for a teacher to commit in such a situation would be not to inform the museum that the group was not coming. By omitting this elementary courtesy valuable time is wasted and another party who might have welcomed the opportunity of even a last minute visit are denied it and ill will may take the place of friendly cooperation.

How often?

How often a class should visit a museum depends almost entirely upon individual circumstances. There are many situations in which it may not be practicable for a class to pay more than a single visit. When distances are very great or travel arrangements exceptionally difficult, a single visit counts as a special treat and such a red letter occasion will probably remain in the children's imagination so that they will want to return on their own when opportunity offers. Obviously it will be invaluable to add to the interest of the single visit by borrowing good visual material, either from the museum or from elsewhere, for display in school and to invite someone to come into the classroom and talk about a related subject.

It is usually best if it can possibly be arranged for a group to pay a series of visits and not only one. A first introduction to a new building, new personalities and new exhibits is bound to be exciting and a little confusing and even the interest of a new bus, coach or train journey may overshadow the more serious purpose of the exercise. However carefully planned the arrangements may

29

be, the children are bound to be keyed up and their attention diffused, at least during the beginning of the visit. But if a series of visits can be arranged and the boys and girls know what they are returning to next time they can think over and discuss what they have seen and there is time between one visit and the next for impressions to build up, for excitement to settle down and any nervousness to be forgotten. A series of four visits is much more than four times as valuable as one single visit; the latter can so easily seem merely an outing, however much those responsible may plan to the contrary. A series of visits to the same place is very clearly a study.

Of course if a number of children are to be taken out three or four times, this may often mean that others will be deprived of a visit and will have to stay in school. This is an important point to consider as it has far reaching implications.

Some teachers think it is fairer if every child can pay one visit to the museum during its school lifetime rather than fewer children paying several. True, each boy and girl will then have had an introduction to the museum but on the other hand none will have enjoyed or understood in any depth. If your purpose is to cultivate an interest and provide a chance for follow up work then it is debatable whether this will best be achieved by providing a relatively superficial experience for many or a fuller one for a few. Bush telegraph operates in these matters among children as much as among adults and nothing whets the appetite so much as hearing how greatly your friend or your desk neighbour have enjoyed their visit out. Probably there is no general answer and each individual answer must be left to the good sense and initiative of the teachers concerned.

How long to stay?
Sufficient time is absolutely essential for a successful visit. Time to take in and become accustomed to strange surroundings, time for chat as well as time for quiet appreciation, time for a gathering together of impressions. Nothing takes away a child's enjoyment of a visit more than a sense of being bustled about. Individual circumstances will largely determine how long you spend on a museum visit, but it is essential to cut your coat according to your cloth and not try to cram too much into the time you have.

Nowadays we all suffer from a damaging sense of hurry. It is difficult to counteract this influence for our children and to give them any sense of mental ease but it is important to try. A museum is one of the places in which quiet looking and time to stand and stare is possible and indeed needed. All museum exhibits, all pictures in an art gallery, are worthy of more than a momentary glance and if you plan your visits carefully with due attention given to preparation, method and duration, then your children will be in a receptive state of mind and perfectly able to look.

Money matters

Sometimes teachers' wishes and intentions concerning visits to museums and other places of interest are subjected to financial considerations of the cost per child, as if one could possibly judge the value of this or that experience to a child in terms of money.

Of course money matters and in education, as in everything else, there have to be priorities. But the race is to the swift and it is the most zealous, most determined and most ingenious teacher whose plans will succeed in the end. It is definitely not cheaper to send forty children in a bus to see something which only some twenty can really see and enjoy and it is essential to plan your visits in *educational* rather than financial terms.

If the school's allocation for visits is already used up then you should think of other ways of finding the money. Nowadays most children have enough pocket money to spare and will readily save up for a fare. Many would be willing to take on some extra work and pay for their visit in that way; others could organize a jumble sale, a raffle or a sweepstake. Collecting and organizing for the visit will be a challenge and the visit itself all the more appreciated. If you yourself do your homework and are more concerned with the quality of the experience for each child than with packing in as many as possible, there is every chance that everyone concerned will get real value for their money and that the children will cherish their introduction to the museum and relive it for a very long time.

Chapter four

What can they do when they get there?

Obviously we want them to look, to look with real interest and enjoyment, with real delight and with some growing measure of understanding. And we want them to question—both verbally and in their own minds—to build upon what they have seen and to ask about anything that occurs during their visit. But children cannot look at things for too long at a time as this is both physically and mentally tiring. Interest will be renewed if some different approach is used at intervals and this interest will be reinforced if they are given opportunities of handling, drawing and discussing objects.

Handling exhibits

Where at all possible, boys and girls will enjoy handling exhibits, appraising their materials, their shape, their texture and their workmanship by direct physical contact. They will be thrilled if they can feel a fabric, run their fingers over a carving, work a spinning wheel, try on a hat or a jacket, carry a sword, strike a note on some previously unknown musical instrument, stroke a bird's feather or the fur of a strange animal. Our hands are very much a part of ourselves; we say that seeing is believing but handling often brings us still nearer the truth. Children in particular enjoy and learn enormously from things they can touch and handle in a museum collection.

However many museum exhibits are too precious, too rare and too fragile to be handled by visitors except in very special circumstances. They have to be preserved and kept for future generations to look at and learn from. Direct physical contact with them is therefore usually impossible for the public.

Many museums have a supply of reserve material in their store rooms which they do not display but which can be put at the disposal of those who ask for it. These may be second rate objects, perhaps slightly broken, faded or worn or good copies of originals

Wearing even a reproduction costume helps to give the feel of a period and drawing the costume fixes the impression.

The best way to find out about a tinder box is to use it oneself.

which although of minor importance to the specialist are full of interest for the uninformed visitor. Or they may simply be duplicates, things not difficult to come by but as significant and interesting in themselves as their prouder relations displayed in the museum galleries.

Even if the authorities of the local museum have had no thought of making this kind of exhibit available for school use, it may well be worth your while to enquire and ask perhaps for favoured treatment and in this way sow the seeds of a regular service of this kind. Teachers know how very useful such material can be to their children and many museum directors and curators do already provide facilities. Others who perhaps know little of education below the specialist level may need persuasion before they will be willing to allow visiting children to see and handle even specimens of lesser importance. They only need to have the different point of view explained to them with perhaps some special pleading or dramatic emphasis and they will in most cases cooperate. It is up to teachers to make an effort on behalf of their children and in all probability a demand will create a supply.

Working models

In a number of museums certain exhibits are arranged so that they can be set in motion by pushing a button or some such simple device. This push button technique is undoubtedly very attractive to children and when used well can be a valuable means of learning. Any teacher should look carefully at anything that children enjoy for there may be a lesson in it for all concerned.

The bustle and excitement engendered by a display of working models does make a museum seem lively and that in itself is important. There are however many different ways of creating a lively atmosphere and it seems important to consider here whether pushing a button is of any real educational value. It requires no effort, makes no demand upon him who pushes, there is usually no choice involved, no selection of material, and therefore no real participation or thought. Indeed if children are given opportunities to push buttons the result can be the very reverse of educational unless the whole exercise is very carefully controlled and the teacher knows exactly what he is aiming at.

What happens so often in a museum is that the children get

33

over excited by working models. They rush from one case to another, pushing the buttons, noticing that a movement has begun but normally not stopping to study it, not reading any label or title, not even questioning the purpose of the machine or whether its operation in real life is controlled by a push button or by some other very different operation. Their interest is often purely superficial, hasty and unlikely to lead to understanding or to any aesthetic or intellectual appreciation.

One armed bandits and other pin table amusements are very much with us these days, but it would seem unnecessary to try to bring this type of exercise into schooling.

It is not suggested that teachers should never make use of such mechanical techniques as pushing buttons, moving levers and so on. Making models is obviously of enormous value and interest to some children. Models to look at can also give a vivid impression of a scene or of how a machine works so long as truth, relevance and accuracy are kept in mind. But it is when boys and girls are surrounded by models which they can set in motion that they become over stimulated, noisy and utterly thoughtless. Like most things push buttons can be used to good or bad effect.

Note taking

All museums contain facts which can be interesting to children and are useful additions to other source material, so note taking is an obvious activity that suits some children. But there is a danger here too. Sometimes boys and girls are so anxious to write notes that they hardly see the exhibits; they scan the labels and notices as if that were the purpose of their visit.

With children of a certain age it is useful to discuss this point and to advise them upon the most fruitful use of their spare time in the museum. Perhaps one or two members of the group can be appointed as note takers while others look through publications on sale and decide upon what might be most useful for the common purpose. As always there can be no set pattern provided that everyone is encouraged to look at the exhibits they have come to see.

Group dynamics

Drawing

Facilities for drawing are provided in many museums and visiting children are sometimes given stools or cushions to sit on and boards, paper, pencils, crayons and rubbers to use. When the museum does not lend this equipment it is essential that teachers should see that their children bring what is necessary with them so that they can draw during their visit.

Drawing is one of the most appropriate and satisfying means of recording a visual experience. Most children enjoy it; their eyes have travelled round the object they have drawn and so it is likely that they will have really looked at it. They return to school with a pictorial reminder and the fact that the picture is their own adds greatly to its value in their eyes and those of their family and friends. To all but a very exceptional child pictures convey very much more than words; all of us tend to draw a diagram or a map on paper or in the air to make our meaning clearer.

But here too we need to take care and to think. We need to remind ourselves of the purpose of the children's drawings and not to lay too great stress upon accuracy of representation. If a boy or girl wants an exact picture, a reminder of an Elizabethan doublet, a silver dish, a Saxon bracelet or an eagle in flight, there are museum postcards or booklets to buy. But a personal drawing is different, less exact probably but it reminds children keenly of the day when they paid that visit and shows them what they saw and what they remembered.

The child who can't draw is often only lacking in confidence. If we can be casual about the matter and suggest that our purpose is for him to look carefully at the object and to record what he sees as best he can but that we do not expect a finished work of art, he may relax and try and carry home his result as proudly as the others. If he does not respond to friendly encouragement then he can make notes instead and you may well discover that he finds his notes less attractive than his friends' sketches and will try drawing next time.

It is so easy to kill a child's interest and reduce his confidence by telling him that his drawing is not right. Rather suggest that he looks again. Pick up the object and ask casually 'which part looks widest here?' and 'can you see the way the deeper carving in the wood looks darker?' and he will look back at his own drawing with new eyes and try a little more. We want at all costs to retain the fresh and spontaneous vision children have but there is room for more careful looking and recording. Educational thought changes in these matters. Free expression used to be in vogue as a reaction against earlier more arid copying. Both can be unfortunate—common sense and an awareness of what is best in each kind of situation where neither the child's ego nor the object's shape is paramount probably gets us all further in the end.

Dramatization

Acting out events with the aid of museum exhibits is a vivid way of bringing museum material to life. Costume, armour, small items of domestic equipment are put at the disposal of school groups in a few museums and add much to the interest and reality of the exhibits. Sometimes curators may be persuaded to lend material for such purposes if a teacher knows what he or she wants and how it can best be used and the result is always good. Any object we wear, use, work with or manipulate comes alive to us as if it were a well known daily companion.

In such cases tact and great care will be necessary, for any breakages will do untold harm, not only to the exhibit itself but to future chances of such opportunities and to the cooperation from which they spring. Care will be needed to ensure that over enthusiastic, over curious hands do not cause damage and that other visitors are not disturbed by the noise and excitement that such activity is sure to bring.

Music and reading

The smell and the sound of any period or place are as much part of its essence as the appearance and the facts about it. Museums can do little about reminiscent smells which might alienate the affection of the visitors, but sound can be used in many ways. Ethnographical museums tend to allow visitors to play on their instruments. Some small history museums like their instruments to be played and the Victoria and Albert Museum has a splendid juke box of period music played on period instruments. Electronics can help visitors to hear music from far off places or periods far more cheaply if a record player can be installed centrally, and speakers in various galleries can be turned on and off. To hear a piece by Byrd in a seventeenth century room, or Beethoven's *Für Elise* in a Victorian one seems to make the furniture glow and the ghosts of the period tiptoe in.

The sound of words can bring a display to life. Margaret Paston's charming love letters to her husband John, Pepys' description of Nancy coming in to announce the fire, Collingwood's dispatch from the *Victory* announcing Nelson's death—whether they are personal, official or imaginative matters little, these words echo across the years and take the visitor back to a very different time. Reading may not have a large part to play in a museum but a part it certainly can have.

Worksheets

A few museums have gone a stage further along the road to personal participation by the child and provide a variety of visual and practical material for school groups. Generally such material consists of guided activity, drawings made round a suggested theme, paragraphs to complete, material to correlate, identify or assemble.

There are many different ways of using such material and building upon the child's enjoyment of doing something. Each activity must depend entirely upon the museum material, the age and type of the children concerned and the past experience and particular skill and bias of the teacher in the museum. If nothing practical for the children to do is provided by the museum, then the teacher taking the group will almost always find it worthwhile to devise something suitable beforehand.

Only two generalizations can be made on this topic. Firstly the material for the children's use must be of a good standard, well thought out, well prepared and pleasant to use. If we aim at a visual impression then we need to bear in mind the visual standard of our tools. It is no good to praise the workmanship and design of a Chippendale chair if the children are provided with dirty, tatty stools to sit on, rough scraps of paper to draw on and gimcrack coathooks or cupboards to hold their overcoats. Standards matter in everything or they do not matter at all.

Secondly visual material used as an incentive to finding out and recording an experience we have enjoyed is generally of greater educational value the further removed it is from a questionnaire or quiz. There is a danger that those who agree that something to do is an important part of any museum visit for children may think of that something in terms of a list of questions to be answered to test how many facts the children have remembered.

Teachers need to look initially at the kinds of question that are asked in a museum context and to decide whether they are right for their children. Mere verbal questions in printed or duplicated form can be of some value provided they are not overdone and that the findings are discussed afterwards. They can certainly help to discourage any vague wandering about on the part of the children. There are however considerable dangers. Unless you are very careful in your choice of questions, the children will look for their answers on the labels or notices rather than looking at and considering the exhibits. It is in the text that verbal, factual answers can be found. Then again they can copy a short written answer from one another without necessarily understanding anything of it. Even if the answer is understood, it will probably be forgotten because words do not impinge upon the average child's mind in the vivid way images do.

But if the activity devised for them consists largely in drawing or in completing drawings, in cutting out or in some other way assembling material to make a coherent statement, the child's effort is necessarily far more his own and the impression gained is likely to be individual and lasting.

A direct factual question demands a direct factual answer. It need involve little analysis or further thought and leaves no room—at least not in a short line on a page—for shades of opinion or emphasis. If we try to answer verbal questions verbally everything tends to be reduced to black and white—this thing comes either from here or from there, it was used by this kind of person but not by that, it is made either of this material or of that, its purpose was either this one or that one and so on. We are in the realm of analysis which seeks security in the belief that everything is either right or wrong. Children *are* like this but adults surely have a responsibility to wean them gradually to a more realistic and tolerant view.

The most far seeing teachers in our schools bring this tolerance into their teaching and it is not difficult to train children for this type of thinking if we use museum material with its non factual aspects foremost in our minds. No examples can perhaps make the point quite clear, for it is entirely a matter of approach and of emphasis, but it does seem when one looks at many museum visitors with their noses stuck in their catalogues, that they think of the exhibits as paragraphs in a text book or entries in a dictionary rather than as exciting and beautiful things to discover, enjoy, admire, think about and discuss. The contrary danger is a woolly sentimentality which leaves everything to intuition and inspired guesswork.

Educational theory swings pendulum like and inevitably some people only catch on to a trend and see the sense of a new idea when that idea has had at least part of its day and healthy reaction has set in. This has happened with the new idea of the importance of self expression rather than formal discipline and control. In the museum context this viewpoint did at one time stress the value of pure contemplation whereby children were left to look at whatever attracted them without adult interference or help. But any experienced teacher knows what is likely to happen if boys and girls are left to contemplate this or that work of art or craft. Unless appropriate links are devised and interpretation offered, the result will almost certainly be a disaster.

One further reason for providing visual material for children to work on when they are taken to see things is that a picture, a model, a chart or any other form of visual statement remains alive long after the visit is over. They can look at it tomorrow, talk about it with their friends, take it home to show mother. It becomes a piece of what they have seen and because they have made it they take special pride in it. By showing it to other people there is proof that the visit has been interesting and therefore encourages them to go when they can. It would be an odd child who felt the same pride and achievement in taking home the answers to twelve questions and an extremely odd mother who was able to show the same enthusiasm and interest in a written page as she would in Tommy's drawing or Mary's model or appliqué figures.

Warnings
The teacher who is keen to make use of museum resources for the benefit of boys and girls needs to bear in mind that museums are not there primarily to serve schools. This is one of the important aspects of their work and has recently been receiving more attention but a museum's primary purpose which is preservation and display must not be hampered by the services it offers for schools. Without such purposes a museum would no longer *be* a museum.

Enthusiasm and keenness can sometimes lead a teacher to assume a little too much in this respect. Of course enthusiasm helps the children and leads to a fuller understanding and appreciation in their learning, but this same enthusiasm needs to be tempered with courtesy and with a sympathetic awareness of other aspects of museum work which may appear relatively unimportant to the layman.

The behaviour of boys and girls when they are in a public building is very much their teacher's responsibility. It is not unknown for children to be left too much to their own devices when visiting a museum in a group. They go over the barriers, touch the exhibits without permission, make an unreasonable degree of noise and eat sweets, sandwiches or even oranges while walking round. When facilities for meals or snacks are not available, some definite arrangement must be made before the children are allowed to eat what they have brought. If you ask for a room to be put at the disposal of your class this can usually be arranged but even then it is quite unpardonable for a boy or girl to drop crumbs, sweet papers, orange peel or any other debris. As a nation we behave abominably in this respect and our streets and public parks are a national scandal. Teachers and parents have considerable responsibility for this.

Nothing but good can come if a child feels that he goes to a museum or art gallery as a privilege rather than as a right and if a special standard of behaviour is expected on these occasions, then the everyday standard will be improved.

As in all things, balance and variety are essential in planning a group visit out of school. The teacher seeking the best results needs only to be on the side of the children in the matter, to know something of the museum exhibits, to cooperate with the museum staff as much as possible and to keep in mind that learning and enjoyment very often go hand in hand.

Chapter five

What can they do afterwards?

A museum visit is not an end in itself any more than is a museum exhibit. Both have a social as well as an aesthetic and an intellectual content and are means towards greater understanding, wider sympathies and increased visual delight—in fact, towards the creation of better and more sensitive people.

Class visits must not be separated from the child's general experience and understanding. If a visit is thought of and dealt with in isolation it loses its potential value as it will almost certainly be forgotten and might as well never have taken place. We have considered the preparations necessary for a group visit and some aspects of what can usefully happen during the visit; it now remains to deal with the next stage of the experience—follow up work.

Writing

It used to be quite common to hear a conscientious teacher say to a group of children leaving a museum: 'Now come along children, we must hurry back to school and write a composition about it all.' One felt keenly for the children and wondered often whether any real interest or appreciation could possibly survive such a dreary, routine form of revision. Yet those who said these words had something of the right idea.

The average child does need to *do* something about what he has seen and heard and enjoyed, if it is to fall into place in his mind and become a worthwhile part of his experience. If he has enjoyed his visit, he will welcome the chance to recreate it in some way. Nowadays the fact that boys and girls are far less often set the task of writing a composition indicates a considerable change in thought and practice. Creative writing is enjoyable for many children if they are encouraged to express themselves freely. Producing an illustrated guide book to a museum they have visited, or a newspaper reporting the day's happenings or writing a play or a poem about people or events seen in a painting, can all be valuable group activities. Writing is an exciting experience for some and a valuable discipline for all but for many children the most they will cheerfully undertake is a letter of thanks or a request for further information. And these are sometimes unbelievably imaginative and charming.

Talk
What else can they do when they get back to school? Of course they will talk about what they have seen and done and there will be little need to arrange or organize this! Such spontaneous talk is very valuable, particularly when it is used for discussion in both large and small groups. There will be many opportunities for the teacher to fill in the gaps in the children's understanding not by direct instruction but by informal reminders. They themselves will teach one another too, for each will have been struck by different things during their visit and by sharing their memories each gains from the others.

There will also be opportunities for those who have been on the visit to recount what they have seen to other groups who have stayed in school. When they have enjoyed themselves they will want to talk about it and when we have something worth recounting we all talk well, so the more they talk after their visit, the better. Where there is a difficulty over the size of the class, it can sometimes be split into two halves to visit different but related places of interest; reports, comparisons and discussions afterwards will certainly enhance the value for everybody. Public speaking is an important skill which can be very useful in life but has to be learnt; the more naturally it is learnt the better.

Reproducing
Talk is one way of reliving and reproducing an experience but there are others and many of them are very attractive to young people. Nowadays in school boys and girls are far busier than they used to be—teachers tend to instruct less and pupils learn more and more by doing. So to many children it will seem quite natural that some kinds of activity follow from a group visit out of the classroom; they will *want* to reproduce what they have enjoyed seeing.

42

Drawing, painting, modelling, puppetry, acting, embroidery, appliqué work in various materials—in fact any form of major or minor craft can be used as an interesting and attractive way of describing their visits and making a permanent record of them. Some of their work will be individual, their own booklets, charts, models and so on but group work is also very valuable as an expression of what has been a group experience and here each child can contribute along the lines he chooses.

What sort of activity should be tackled and where does craft come in? Every teacher will see different possibilities in every museum, art gallery or historic house. The following extract from a series of leaflets issued by the Geffrye Museum with folders of photographs may give additional ideas.

Ideas for follow up work

The material in this folder can be used in a variety of ways. If your children have visited and discussed the Stuart Room in the Geffrye Museum, they will enjoy taking a further, more careful look and reliving the experience of handling genuine objects, dressing up in reproduction costume and listening to period music. If they have not visited us, these photographs can introduce them to a middle class English home of the seventeenth century and give a vicarious feel of the period. Specific suggestions which may be of help in using the material:

1 The photographs could be displayed in the library, surrounded by appropriate story and reference books.

2 The children could draw and paint pictures, make model rooms in shoe boxes, bowls and jugs in clay, appliqué pictures of a room and people, costume dolls, period puppets and marionettes. They could also embroider a period design on a more substantial cover for this folder.

3 These photographs, and those which we plan to produce for other periods, can form the basis of pictorial time charts, to be built up either by individuals or groups.

4 There is material here for making and acting plays, discussion, and writing stories and poems.

5 Reproductions of objects used daily in the seventeenth century home can be made by the children—a bowl of dried petals and spices to make a pot pourri; a candle made by dipping a wick

many times into melted fat; a piece of woodcarving, fabric printing or sewing, using seventeenth century motifs.

6 Collections of postcards and pictures are more meaningful if they are based on a theme—what people wore, what occupations they followed, what furniture they used and so on. Children can enjoy this kind of detective work when they visit museums.

7 An exploration of the locality can also provide exciting follow up detective work; museums and country houses show pictures many of which give details of costume and family life; inn signs and shop signs often have interesting clues; church registers add local names to the list of more famous people; antique shops often show good examples of furniture and domestic utensils; local crafts sometimes echo everyday work of the past; there may even be local sources of customs and games like bowls and archery.

8 Older children can make costumes of the period with the help of *Patterns of Fashion: English Women's Dresses and their Construction* by Janet Arnold. A wig hired from a theatrical costumier would complete the outfit. To a child dressed in costume, the taste of freshly ground coffee and hot drinking chocolate in seventeenth century business houses can provide historical insight.

9 Country children can be encouraged to find history in the hedgerows and gardens; many of the herbs, plants and flowers which were used so extensively in seventeenth century textiles and tapestries are still growing and can be collected, drawn, pressed or used in decoration.

10 A parents' 'Open Evening' at the end of the exercise showing work based on the photographs will help to foster interest and add purpose and excitement to family outings to museums and historic houses, both at home and abroad.

Exhibition

A series of visits to a museum to study a particular theme can be a useful focal point for various kinds of practical work before, during and after the visits, and can interest the whole school and neighbourhood if what the children have made is assembled in the form of an exhibition.

This is a way of making sure that boys and girls of very varied capacities all play a part; the group approach often encourages a backward or diffident child who might not feel able to produce anything worth while entirely on his own. Such mundane tasks as sticking the drawings onto charts or making a list of what is displayed have to be done by somebody and it is an important lesson for all to learn that such details can make or mar the whole and that therefore it is not only the star performers who deserve praise.

Such a small exhibition is important from the point of view of the rest of the school. Those who have not been able to share in the visit have their interest aroused and gain something from the experience of the more fortunate ones and they may perhaps be encouraged to explore on their own or with their parents.

Parents, Governors and others interested in the work of the school will be pleased to be invited to see the display and will be persuaded—if persuasion be needed—that learning can happen as fruitfully out of school as in the classroom.

Many boys and girls in the class will probably enjoy acting as guides and their practice in explaining matters to visitors will be good for them and good too for the reputation of the school.

Assessment

To the teacher who has organized the visits and the head who has facilitated and arranged time for it, there would appear to be only two valid criteria by which the exercise can be judged. The two are dependent upon one another: firstly, have Johnny and Mary enjoyed their visit and secondly, are they likely to return again on their own? It is really only the first point that needs to be considered, for we can be absolutely certain that return they will at some time or another if the visit has been worth while.

It is always the free individual action that matters most—the voluntary audience rather than the captive one. If we can help our young people while they are still at school to enjoy exploring the amenities of their environment, when they are grown up they will know how to use the increased leisure time which inevitably will be theirs.

Chapter six

Where else can they go?

Granted that museums are worthwhile places for young people to visit and that there are various educational methods which can bring museum exhibits to life for even relatively dull children, are there other places equally worth visiting? Very many schools have no museum in their neighbourhood and are looking for an alternative; others perhaps have used their local museum very considerably and have found that learning out of school can be a lively and enriching experience. They are anxious to explore further—where can they go?

It is tempting to say 'anywhere out of the classroom'. Although we know that lively teachers are much more important to children than fine buildings, the dreary buildings in which many boys and girls still have to spend their most impressionable years must have a harmful effect. Not only are these old school buildings physically cramped and lacking in basic amenities but they are so often dark and dreary with nothing to stimulate the senses. Almost anywhere is better than such a place.

However, gay posters can enliven drab walls and a coat or two of bright paint can work wonders. If these cannot be provided officially, there are schools in some areas where parents, teachers, older boys and girls organize evening work parties and bring a new look to old walls. But to feel a real sense of release from the restraints of past architectural styles the children need to go out of the school.

Teachers know best what their children will enjoy and it is impossible to generalize; in fact the only purpose in including this chapter at all is to give a little encouragement to any teacher who may not yet have experienced the interest and variety that school visits can bring.

Information in the classroom

You must know what is going on in your district. You need to have contact with all the people and places that can offer something useful and interesting, so your name must be on mailing lists. A 'What's On' board in the school displayed in some prominent place and kept up to date can be a focal point of interest and discussion.

Art galleries and museums, art dealers, stores, craft workshops and social clubs usually have a mailing list and all will welcome a request from a teacher for a name to be added. Some newspapers and journals publish weekly or monthly diaries with lists of concerts, exhibitions, meetings and so on which can be cut out and mounted and a board displaying all this information can be a constant reminder to staff and children alike that even the most unpromising neighbourhood offers something worth seeing or hearing to those who seek.

Looking around

Do not think only of exhibitions, displays and things intended for the interest of visitors; there are many other things worth looking at and valuable for your children. Buildings of all kinds have a fascination if we have learnt how to read them and a walk down the street can stimulate discussion on so many things—geographical, historical, aesthetic, ethical, mathematical even though it is sad that one has to use words which imply that these different facets are different subjects. A historic house, an old cottage, a church, even a graveyard—these can all be used for stimulation, enjoyment, understanding, comparison and as incentives to further exploration and activity. They can all be either starting points, signposts or links for we need to remember that nothing can profitably be studied in isolation. Boys can learn enormously from watching a building being constructed if their teacher interprets the experience and uses it fully. Girls can be equally stimulated if they go shopping with specific aims and criteria in mind, and follow it up with discussion afterwards. (See Schools Council Working Paper No 11 for examples of work of this kind.)

There are few limits to the type of visits that can be valuable provided the teacher's approach is far seeing and the visit is sensibly organized. Youngsters need to be introduced to any sphere or place where they can catch a glimpse of new and interesting aspects of life both past and present, national and international, man made and natural, and similarly anywhere where they can get first hand experience and find new nourishment for their minds and their imaginations. This is particularly important for the early leavers, those boys and girls who are going to jump suddenly from school to adult life with little to help them face the differences.

Teacher as guide

Sometimes there will be a guide at a special exhibition, or historic house, or a friendly vicar in your village church, who will give the children an introductory talk about the building and its contents. It will be a good idea if you can suggest tactfully that the talk should be short with opportunity for questions after the children have looked around. There is nothing worse than a guided tour unless superlatively done.

In many cases you will have to cope with the interpretation yourself and many teachers tend to feel diffident about taking boys and girls to see something which they themselves know little or nothing about. Such diffidence is fully understandable and indeed wise, but if its effect is to deny to the children a worthwhile experience then surely it is misplaced.

Any teacher wondering whether he or she dare take a class to this or that exhibition needs to think less in terms of getting information from what is seen than in essentially different terms of setting light to an interest and stimulating the imagination. Of course you yourself must have some idea of what the exhibition is about and you must know clearly why you think the children should see it. It may help you to know where and when this painter lived, what materials this sculptor uses, where other paintings by the same artist can be seen and so on but only so that you can ask and answer questions that arise and not so that you can deliver a talk about these matters.

The more you yourself know of this background information, the more confident you will be and the more enthusiasm and enjoyment your children will feel. You need to know when to ask a question, make a comment or add an allusion which can bring right home to the children the connection between what they are seeing and their own everyday life and experiences. If we approach an exhibition of painting and sculpture with a spirit of adventure

History, art and geography combine to make a collage of the Pipe of Peace after a visit to a museum.

An Elizabethan lady shows how even newspaper can be used imaginatively.

and enjoy it and find out its secrets *with* the children rather than with any sense of what they ought to learn from it and what we ought to teach them, then the visit will in all probability be a memorable one.

I am neither an artist nor an art historian, but I remember many occasions when the fresh viewpoint and lively comments of boys and girls have helped me to see and enjoy a picture more fully than I might otherwise have done and to understand a little more of the artist's meaning. As in every sphere of life, understanding and appreciation grow if we can grasp a person's purpose and intentions. So one sometimes starts off by asking 'why do people paint?' We discuss this, and discuss means mainly collecting ideas and impressions from the children and collating them outside the exhibition room before we go in. After five minutes we come to the conclusion that there are many different reasons for painting a picture but that one of the most important is that the artist wants to tell us, through his picture, something which he feels is important. So we shall agree to approach his work in a spirit of enquiry and discovery with at least a part of our eyes and minds open for what he has to say to us.

But before we go in there are a few practical signposts which may be helpful such as a word or two perhaps about the particular pictures we are going to see—they are by a number of artists who have painted and drawn in many countries in Europe during the past 700 years, they are all by the same person, perhaps a man who settled a few years ago in a coal mining district and who now sees much of interest and even of beauty in his surroundings; they are by a woman who uses cloth and buttons and other everyday materials to make pictures as delicate and as full of meaning as the most careful water colour painting—this is a tuning up stage and it should not last too long.

Then we go in. Allow five or ten minutes to look round, depending upon the age, interest and behaviour of the children. Anyone with a sense of the ripe moment will know when to gather them together by suggesting 'who has a favourite one, let's go and look at that', or 'let's look at this one first' or even 'is there one you don't understand or don't like'. We all sit down in front of the picture, on the floor if necessary for dusty pants distract far less from aesthetic appreciation and interest than tired legs and scuffing feet. We look for a moment without speaking then someone probably makes a comment and we lead on from that, or one breaks in oneself with a suitable question perhaps 'do you think he enjoyed painting it?' or 'I wonder where he was when he painted it' or 'I wonder how he felt' or 'have you ever seen anything like that?' or 'is it a picture you would like to have at home or not?' or 'I wonder how he got the feeling of heat, or coolness, or quiet, or storminess, or sadness into the picture' and so on. It matters little enough which picture you are looking at or whether the children differ greatly from one another in their attitudes, as indeed they almost certainly will. What matters is that they should really look at a picture, they should get a glimpse of the fun and the challenge of seeing a fine thing and catch from you something of an open minded and receptive approach to works of art.

Looking at anything can be fun, whether it is exhibited specially to be looked at or not. Churches, houses, streets, wharfs, bridges, all these and other places too come alive if one can train one's eyes and therefore the children's, to look at them enquiringly with a critical as well as an appreciative eye and see them in the context of their particular time and place without hurrying by too quickly. This question of the context of what we look at is important but difficult because some children will find it easier to concentrate on the facts before them than imagine a building's original context and will quickly become restless.

Preparing to travel
This difference between individuals is particularly noticeable in those who travel. Some like to read as much as they can beforehand about the district to which they are going, pore over maps and find out the geography, history and sometimes even the geology and social structure of the place they are visiting; they get most enjoyment out of their visit if they prepare themselves factually. Others like to go without too much mental baggage so as to let the first impressions be visual and emotional and then perhaps to read about it all afterwards. The former may suffer from over intensity and concentrate so much upon the factual side of things that they can scarcely bear to take their eyes off their guide books; the latter may perhaps see more brightly as a result of their more haphazard approach and they will experience the

pleasurable shock of things seen unexpectedly, but they will often be assailed with a sense of their own ignorance and may wish that they had read more beforehand.

Children differ just as much in these matters and it is as well to discuss the different attitudes with them and to allow for a variety of approaches. We want to encourage them to travel with their eyes and minds wide open and this is of increasing importance now that children whose parents never had the chance are beginning to travel. Perhaps the value of your sallies out of the classroom can only be fully assessed in a generation's time when the boys and girls now in your care are taking their own children abroad.

A warning

If you are an out of school visit enthusiast do beware of attempting too much at a time. Sometimes you may be tempted to arrange more than one visit in the course of a day or several in a week. It is not unknown for a group of children to be taken to two, three, or even four different museums or exhibitions on one day. The motive is often blameless—there are so many interesting things to see, time is limited and money even more so, and since a coach has to be hired for the journey it seems best to fit in as much as possible.

Such an arrangement is absolutely useless; in fact it is worse than useless for it serves only to prejudice everyone concerned and make them determined, subconsciously at any rate, not to visit those places again. The same dangers which hamper anyone who tries to see more than one museum on one occasion also beset anyone who tries to see a whole museum in a single visit. If you have to go far to your visit, then perhaps you can deal successfully with one place in the morning and a second in the afternoon, but never never more than two and only then if they complement one another or provide a useful contrast. Even then you will need to plan for a lengthy lunch time, provide opportunities to sit and chatter or to run round and play and ensure a smooth journey home to avoid everyone being worn out and unhappy. All those concerned with class visits need to remember the relationship between bodily comfort and ease and intellectual and emotional appreciation and enjoyment.

Chapter seven

Special schools go out also

Many people who accept that museum visits can be interesting and enjoyable for the average child, tend to think that they are unnecessary for those of higher intelligence and useless for the handicapped.

Both points of view show a very limited understanding of the possibilities. Boys and girls who learn mainly through books can gain a great deal of interest and understanding from contact with real things, and those who are handicapped and lack confidence and human contacts can also be much helped by visual, practical experience. Some museums do receive parties from special schools and many more would be willing to do so if teachers were to ask for help and for the special arrangements which have to be made for such groups.

In a book called *Changing Museums* (Longmans 1967) I have written about museum visits for handicapped boys and girls:

> *Many of the outside interests which the majority of children are encouraged to pursue are of course beyond the capacity of the majority of handicapped children. Yet they are able to take advantage of much that used to be closed to them. Libraries often make arrangements for such children and they can and do enjoy visiting museums if their special needs can be foreseen and kept in mind.*

> *Curiosity in human beings is not confined to any one sense and those who have not eyes to see, or ears to hear with, or whose bodies or minds are but partially equipped for understanding, can nevertheless experience wonder and excitement, novelty and awakening interest. Indeed, those less endowed seem often to respond more easily to tangible objects than to words and books.*

> *Tangible is the key word. We say that seeing is believing but tend to forget that touching and feeling may be even more the key to a knowledge of things. Where one sense is absent or atrophied, others seem to be heightened to offset the loss so that,*

given imagination, goodwill and a willingness to adapt and to experiment on the part of all the adults concerned museum visits for all kinds of handicapped children can supply a real need.

Blind children

Preliminary arrangements are important. If your children are blind or partially sighted you will have to tell the museum beforehand, for attendants as well as teaching staff must be told that a special group is expected. Stools or chairs must be placed ready for them and other visitors requested to use other parts of the museum for the time being.

If it is a period room they are going to see, the furniture will have to be rearranged to allow them to follow a set route for exploring it. This route will have to be carefully thought out beforehand and you can obviously be of help to the museum staff in planning this. You will want the children's interest to flow naturally from one object to another. Small objects will have to be put away so that they cannot be knocked over but will be shown later. The museum teacher will go round with the children, one behind the other, talking and questioning as they feel, for example, the rush covered floor, the panelled walls, the wooden shutters and the carved fireplace. They may linger for as long as they wish, exploring with their fingers these typical aspects of a sixteenth century room. Then in twos and threes they discover the larger pieces of furniture, such as chairs, stools and chests.

The essentials are very careful discussion of the problems and very careful preparation of the room; approach in single file giving time for individual exploration and comment and above all maintain a relaxed, friendly atmosphere.

When the boys and girls have returned to their seats the various small objects which help to create the atmosphere of a period room are passed round, handled and discussed. When possible the children are left to discover for themselves what the object is and how it works, for this is exciting. A group of blind seventeen year olds have been enthralled to recreate the atmosphere of an eighteenth century room by tasting china tea and feeling what their teacher 'looked like' in a wig.

While the children's interest is still lively they can be given plasticine and will enjoy making models of what they have 'seen', the work being divided up so that they cover everything between them. At the end of the visit their work is packed up for them to take back to school. Follow up work will, of course, depend upon their own teachers and many interesting projects can develop. The memory of blind youngsters is surprisingly vivid and their highly developed tactile sense enables them to reproduce recognizable details of carving and ornament. Scale seems to be important to them and the most lifelike models are usually of small objects that can be enclosed in the hand.

Deaf children

Deafness is of course not so great a handicap to museum visiting as blindness because the children can see and in fact their vision is often very acute and detailed. They can be encouraged to look closely, provided the teacher uses a clear, slow diction so that they can lip read with ease.

So here too it is important to tell the museum staff about the group's handicap beforehand. Deaf children can get particular enjoyment from participation—seeing and manipulating objects that move, smelling dried herbs, tasting china tea—anything that can help them to use the senses they have and to feel less cut off from other people.

Immigrant children

Language is also the greatest difficulty in dealing with immigrant children. Many teachers realize the importance of helping new-comers to this country to make contacts outside home and school and museums are among the places where links can be shown and new connections made between different countries, different cultures, different social purposes. The museum teacher receiving these boys and girls, just as the class teacher who sees them daily, will need to speak in very simple friendly terms, with an accent upon participation and general discussion. And since some of these first generation immigrants will know little of the normal pattern of social behaviour in this country, valuable lessons can be learned from the way their teacher deals with people on the way to and from the visit. Even a short visit may be a new experience for them and all children learn a great deal by example.

54

ESN children

Museums can serve the educationally subnormal also. The chief difficulties here are the great ability range within a group and the short attention span of the children. The groups must of course be small, the atmosphere sympathetic and brisk, the subject matter simple and the visit not too long. Above all, everyone concerned must feel convinced that the experience is worthwhile for the children in their own terms.

Their potential is very limited, but many of them react at once to visual stimulation; their verbal response is sometimes surprising and some of them are able to make reasoned, if primitive, deductions. They enjoy listening to music and if the museum has records of music—period music, folk music, primitive music, bird song, animal calls—they will be much appreciated. These boys and girls have little understanding of the unfamiliar and no time sense as normal children have, but their enjoyment is keen when they have made models and grouped them so that everyone has helped to make a whole room or scene.

Such a visit calls for adjustment on the part of the museum staff, but they will undoubtedly cooperate willingly if tactfully asked. Much of the value of the visit will be lost unless the class teacher has led up to it carefully and is prepared to build upon the inspiration gained from the experience. It is gratifying to find many devoted teachers in special schools prepared to take the extra trouble and strain involved in helping their children to enjoy some of the extras available to normal boys and girls.

If one believes that one of the most important purposes of any museum is that it should be enjoyed, what more is there to ask? Enjoyment and pleasure are entirely relative terms. The connoisseur and the research student enjoy their museum visits for reasons which are dear to them; the average man, woman or child needs help and encouragement if a visit is to mean very much; help is even more necessary for those who are handicapped. They too can enjoy what a museum has to offer and if their response is judged in relation to their ability they are among the most rewarding of visitors.

Remedial children

There are in our schools large numbers of boys and girls who have no accepted or measurable mental or physical handicap, but who are intellectually handicapped by environmental causes. They are the children described in *Children in Distress* by Clegg and Megson (Penguin 1968). These young people may or may not be poor financially, but they are poor in bearing. They speak poorly, often carry themselves badly, lack confidence and any lustre. It is evident that their lives give them little real pleasure or opportunity for growth and probably their homes are equally deprived. Their fathers may be work shy and shiftless, their mothers incapable and worn down by circumstance and both parents perhaps emotionally inadequate and intellectually undeveloped. Evidence given to the Schools Council in *Society and the Young School Leaver* (Working Paper 11) and to the Newsom Committee in *Half our Future* describes this kind of child: *It is not so much that they are ill mannered, but that many of them have a complete lack of any social skill. . . . Very many of these less gifted young people are socially maladroit, ill at ease in personal relationships, unduly selfregarding and insensitive; their contact even with their peers is often ineffectual. . . . .* Many of them may well appear much more stupid than they are simply because they come from inarticulate homes where there is no conversation worth listening to, where they have for years been told 'shut up' and 'don't ask silly questions' whenever they query anything, and where there are no opportunities for any peace or privacy.

This type of handicap cannot be dealt with by separate provision in special schools for it is a social problem as much as an educational one. It involves parents as much as teachers, it involves all social agencies including museums. All the reasons which make museum collections potentially attractive to other young people make them equally so to those less favoured and all the reasons which often make museums uninviting are more likely to put off the less academic.

Yet they are the majority, they are indeed more than *Half Our Future*.

Chapter eight

Some practical suggestions

It is obviously impossible to make suggestions as to the best use to be made of any particular museum or art gallery for such institutions are very numerous and varied and no teacher can hope to arrange visits beyond a certain distance from the school. The best plan, as suggested in chapter two, will be for the teacher to pay a preliminary visit to the museum to find out what facilities if any are offered to school parties and make plans accordingly.

It might be helpful to outline a few pieces of practical work which have been used with children when visiting a number of places of interest. This kind of individual work encourages observation and has in addition the extra interest that comes from personal, individual compilation. The resulting booklets or series of sheets are often prized and enjoyed and talked about long after the visits themselves.

In order to arrange for such activity the teacher must obviously have looked carefully at the things that the children are going to see; there must be a plan and some means must be devised to duplicate outlines for the children to work on. This kind of invitation to finding out is far more encouraging to most children than drawing on a blank sheet of paper; it has more purpose and is a persuasive way of confining interest to the matter in hand. Of course many other approaches are equally valuable and there can be no set pattern for a successful visit.

A page dealing with decorative aspects of exhibits.

A page of patterns

Carved in wood			
Wrought or cast in metal			
Woven or embroidered or printed on cloth			

This is an extract from a booklet prepared for a visit to a country house.

Prince Henry's room

Now walk upstairs and look round this lovely old room. The ceiling is beautiful and has in the middle a crest which belonged to
. . . .

Imagine yourself a boy or girl of the early seventeenth century visiting this room for the first time. You would see many things which would surprise you. Make a list of them here:

Why would they seem strange?

A page from a booklet entitled *Exploring Eighteenth Century London*.

The Adelphi

In this block of houses you can see that the effect of the whole s........ has been considered before that of each h........

Robert Adam introduced the use of stucco, or plaster ornament, on the outside of houses.

Another typical feature of eighteenth century houses is the use of wrought iron balconies, usually in a very light and delicate design.

Make a drawing of doorway number 8 or 9 showing the beautiful fanlight over the door as well as the ornament:

Draw the balcony you like the best:

You will notice that house number 7 is of a different character from the others, but is still part of the general design, in proportion and ornament. That is, it still takes its place as a *unit* of the whole.

Make a drawing of number 7, or draw the designs used on the flat column faces, and the ornament along the top of the columns.

A page from a booklet which can be used in connection with either a specific exhibition or to link together various visits in a neighbourhood.

I lived in (London) in the ......th century

My name was.........................
....
And I................................
....
....

I dressed like this:

My house was built of ....

with ....

My wife
and I are
eating
our
....

This is how we entertained our friends.

We sometimes travelled like this.

We met or heard about these famous people:

. . . .

. . . .

An extract from a booklet devised in connection with a week's visit of London children to a small country town.

The museum

Section nine
Some of the commonest birds in Britain are sparrow, robin, starling, thrush, blackbird, blue tit, chaffinch. I have ticked those I have seen out of doors and put a star by those I have found in the museum.
These are some more birds I know:.....................
....
Here are sketches of some I should very much like to see out of doors and a note of their colours.

Entrance hall
How many of the wild flowers do you know already?.........
.... Sketch some you would especially like to find.
Make a note of their colours.

Appendix one

Have you thought of everything?

1 A preliminary visit to the museum.
2 The approval of your head.
3 Arrangements about date, time, numbers, theme, with museum staff.
4 Information for parents about date, time, clothing, food, money.
5 Tell the children about the visit and the journey, what they are going to do and why.
6 Arrangements for a coach, or checking train times and connections.
7 Find out where, en route, a child can spend a penny if necessary.
8 Find out where, en route, there is a public telephone.
9 Tablets for those who suffer from travel sickness.
10 Something to do, or look out for, on the journey.
11 Pencils and paper if the museum does not provide them.
12 Find out whether there are publications and refreshments for which children will need money.
13 It is safer to take drinks in polythene or tins than in glass bottles.
14 Those who own cameras may like to know that they can take them.
15 Thank you letters from the children.
16 Write to tell the museum about interesting follow up work.
17 Assess the worth of the visit immediately afterwards and make notes to remind yourself of possible improvements for next time.

A medieval heraldic fringe made of small pieces of screwed up tissue paper.

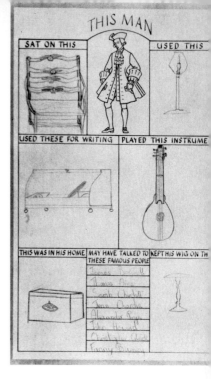

Given specific things to look for in a museum children will enjoy searching for details and by choosing from among a variety of exhibits will build up a picture of a period.

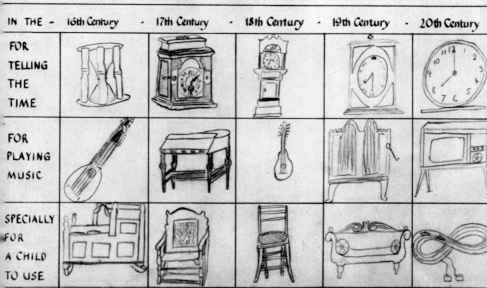

Appendix two

The story of Fred

I am indebted to Sir Alec Clegg for permission to reproduce the opening address he gave in April 1965 to the Annual Conference of the Group for Educational Services in Museums. Nothing could illustrate more simply and more vividly the part that museums can play in the education of our children in this industrial age.

About one hundred years ago there was a small boy called Fred and he lived on an island with his father and mother and nearby lived his uncle and aunt. His father kept pigeons and bees and a garden of flowers and vegetables. His uncle was a forester and planted acre after acre of trees in rows. The boy did not go to school—there wasn't a school on the island—but his mother taught him to read and write and encouraged him to draw and paint pictures. She also recited poetry to him and sang to him when he was little. Every year he went to stay with another uncle who lived in York and had a passion for the history of the city, which he loved to illustrate by its walls, its churches and the objects of history which it contained. He also loved to take his small nephew to Malham and Gordale Scar and tell him about its geography and geology. And the boy, stimulated by these practical interests of his parents and his two uncles, grew up in understanding of many things.

Then one day a learned educationalist visited the island and met the boy and was astonished at his understanding of many things and at the knowledge which he had developed round these things and the educationalist said to himself—How wonderful it would be if every child in the land had the learning which this boy has built around the simple experiences which he has had with bees, pigeons, flowers, vegetables, forestry and a visit to York and Malham. The learned educationalist was amazed to find out how well the boy spoke mainly because his mother read and recited to him and because he himself had read much about the interests which derived from his own personal experiences. And the learned educationalist reasoned thus—It is impossible for every child to lead the life that this boy has led and to develop the knowledge that this boy has without the experiences.

First of all we will look at his numerical and mathematical ability which he has gained from reckoning areas from odd shaped bits of land and working out the number of trees they will take, and from his mother's shopping expeditions, and from the measuring which he has to do in making pigeon lofts and bee hives and we will reduce these to simple symbolic formulae and tables and make children learn a lot of them very quickly.

Then we will take the boy's speech and writing which is so good and subject it to careful analysis and if we teach other boys whose writing and speech is not so good how to subject what they say and write to this kind of analysis they will realize how badly they speak and write and will promptly set about trying to improve the way they speak and write.

Then, said the learned educationalist, we cannot provide every child with the bees and the pigeons and the flowers and vegetables which have taught this boy so much, but we can cause books to be written and force them to learn what is in these books. We will have books written about all that has happened in the history of the city of York and all that is known of the geography and geology of Malham and Gordale, and we will make all boys learn these facts and they will then have the understanding that our original boy had who lived with his father and his uncle on an island.

So the learned educationalist went home and divided out the boy's knowledge into parcels which he called subjects, and he called a lot of clever men called H & S and W & M and D & P and P & R and many others, and handed them a parcel of knowledge and told them to write a book about that parcel.

And then he went to the schools and he said—I have met a very remarkable little boy named Fred who has derived great understanding from his bees and his pigeons, from shopping with his mother and listening to her recite poetry, from visiting and seeing and finding out about all the ancient buildings in York and from trips to Gordale. His understanding of these things has led

66

him to read about them and derive great knowledge of them. What I want you to do is to reverse this process. Give your boys the knowledge that you will find in these books by Messrs H & S, W & M, D & P and P & R and when you give them this knowledge the understanding will follow.

And so it came about that all over the land children were assembled in groups of forty and made to learn the facts set out in the books written by Messrs H & S, W & M, D & P and P & R.

And the learned educationalist began to entertain a horrible suspicion that the reverse process didn't work. In other words, whereas the little boy named Fred grew in understanding because he started with experience and read to feed the interest which derived from it, those who started with the reading failed to develop understanding because the interest was not there. The facts were in a vacuum unrelated to the context of the lives of those who absorbed them.

But the learned educationalist thrust these horrible suspicions aside and said to himself—The facts derived from books are making no impact because they are not properly learned. It is all these inefficient teachers who cannot impart facts that are causing the trouble. What we want is something wherewith to prod the teachers so that they impart more facts efficiently. So he said— We will have external examiners who will set tests to the children to find out whether they have learned the facts. Those who have had facts imparted to them effectively will pass the tests and those who have not will fail to pass the tests, and when the lists are read out on the speech day the incompetence of the bad fact imparters will be revealed to the world and this will act as a goad to make them impart their facts better in future.

But then before any external examinations had taken place the learned educationalist died and he never learned whether or not the sound learning of facts about pigeons and bees and flowers and vegetables and York and Gordale produced the same understanding in the mass of children that practical experience of them had given to Fred on his island with his mother and father and uncle. Fred died as well, but children were still brought together in groups of forty, and Messrs H & S, W & M, D & P and P & R and thousands and thousands of other people all wrote books full of more and more facts, and these were forced into millions of children and the capacity of the children to disgorge them at will was tested by thousands and thousands of examiners hired to do this job by scores of external examining agencies.

And what was entirely forgotten was that all this started in an attempt to give the understanding which derives from experience to those who have never had the experience.

Then it was learned that some could learn more facts more quickly than others and so when children reached the age of eleven they were subjected to a fact learning orgy and those who learned most facts most quickly were creamed off and put into special fact learning places known as grammar schools to the great delight of Messrs H & S, W & M, D & P and P & R.

Then attempts were made to isolate how many facts the average child from average circumstances taught by average teachers in average schools at the average age of eleven should know, and once he was isolated a learned body known as M. House gave him an index mark IQ 100.

Then in 1931 a Government publication known as the Hadow Report on the Primary School made a statement which harked right back to Fred who started all this, by stating that education should be thought of in terms of activity and experience and not in terms of knowledge to be acquired and facts to be stored, but this made no impact whatever on the schools at that time.

However, in due course, a few, a very few indeed, intelligent teachers came to take a cool look at what was happening and they realized that for the vast majority of children the majority of our educational processes add about as much to their mental stature as a diet of sawdust would add to their physical stature.

And things began to happen. Children were less and less told how to do things and were encouraged to do things in their own way. They were given fewer and fewer facts by the teachers and encouraged to find out more and more for themselves. Above all, there was a realization that it is experience rather than factual knowledge which is the springboard to interest and understanding. The problem then arose as to how to give experience to batches of forty, the kind of experience which had produced the understanding in Fred which had first excited the interest of the learned educationalist.

It was decided by these wise teachers that they would keep

pigeons and bees in the school, where they would also grow flowers and vegetables and that they would take the school to visit York and Malham, and that in the meantime they would bring a great variety of material into the classroom. They would bring Roman pottery and glass which the children could handle, they would show models of Roman villas and forts and walls and gates and heating systems, and before the school went to Gordale and when it came back the pupils would see models of the geological formations they were going to visit and they would handle the specimens of the rock they found there.

And in this way many of the pupils in the school gained the understanding which derives from doing and were no longer content with merely remembering what they had read.

Appendix three

Some official viewpoints

Extracts from *Half Our Future*—a report of the Central Advisory Council for Education (HMSO 1963).

In western industrialized countries, the hours which must necessarily be spent in earning a living are likely to be markedly reduced during the working lifetime of children now in school. The responsibility for ensuring that this new leisure is the source of enjoyment and benefit it ought to be, and not of demoralizing boredom, is not the schools' alone, but clearly education can play a key part. A great deal has been written elsewhere about the impact of all the vastly extended means of mass communication and entertainment. Certainly everybody needs, as never before, some capacity to select, if only in the interests of fuller enjoyment, from the flood of experience continually presented. Our pupils, more than most, need training in discrimination. (Paragraph 81)

As well as meeting visitors in school, the pupils themselves need to go out and explore. Sometimes they may go as small teams carrying out a particular investigation. At others they may be taking part in a series of visits planned to give them glimpses of different types of industry or to take them to places of cultural interest. Always they will need good preliminary briefing. Many schools do already arrange excellent programmes of this kind, but there is room for more experiment in this field, especially in relating the experiences of the visits more closely to the rest of the work in school. The pupils themselves ought to be brought in as much as possible to the initial planning and organization and making of arrangements. In the management of themselves and their contacts with other people outside the familiar school situation, and in the subsequent presentation of their experience, they can learn much, quite apart from any specific information they may have acquired. (Paragraph 220)

An education which is practical, realistic and vocational in the sense in which we have used these words, and which provides some ground in which to exercise choice, is an education that makes sense to the boys and girls we have in mind. It should also make sense to the society in which they live and which provides their education. But if their education could be completely described in these words it would be sadly lacking. An education that makes complete sense must provide opportunity for personal fulfilment—for the good life as well as for good living. This is not, of course, a matter for a series of lessons. It is a quality to be sought, not a subject to be taught. One of the elements involved is that which shines out when the only possible answer to the question 'Why are you taking so much trouble to do this properly?' is 'Because I enjoy doing it'. This situation may well arise in the course of a hobby, but it may also be found in parts of school work. Wherever it occurs, it is something to be fostered—doing something worth while for its own sake is a principal aim not only of education but of life. It is within the reach of clever and stupid alike. (Paragraph 328)

Extracts from The Schools Council Working Paper No 11— *Society and the Young School Leaver* (HMSO 1967).

Every teacher knows that the lead into a particular subject must be interesting to the pupils and must be capable of gaining their attention. But this is not the same thing as an approach based on asking the pupils what they 'want to know'. Such an approach has often led to disappointing results in the schools in which it has been tried. It is expecting a lot of 14 year olds to ask them what they want to know. The answers will vary from day to day according to the impact of events in the life of the pupils; many of them think that any subject that is not on their examination syllabus is a waste of time. It is not for them to tell us what to teach; it is our job to seek out methods which work, and they will not work unless they arouse the interest of the pupils. (Paragraph 35)

Most young school leavers are more likely to be interested in vocational subjects. This makes good sense for they will be at work next year. Many schools arrange visits to industrial and commercial premises, and some schools have been experimenting with vocational courses and work experience. Such courses can often contribute to building up that essential minimum of basic knowledge about the world of work which is indispensable to an informed and sensible choice of career. There is no doubt that a course for young school leavers should have an educational basis, but there are some signs that this can be overdone. Work visits without adequate preparation and follow up have sometimes proved unrewarding for the time they take. Many children do have work experience before they leave school in part time jobs and full time employment during the summer holidays. (Paragraph 36)

It is not only in the world of work that the young school leavers will have to be adaptable. Fundamental changes affecting the whole social pattern now occur within the life of a single individual, so we must also teach people how to adapt to ever changing social circumstances. It follows that the ability to go on learning is a more important asset than acquiring a mass of information, some of which will soon be out of date and which is, in any given subject, already of unmanageable dimensions. The main aim of the humanities in particular must be to show the pupils how to learn and to give them an appetite for learning. (Paragraph 38)

Each topic must be relevant and it must appear to the pupils to be relevant; the pupils' desire to find out and explore for themselves should also be encouraged. Instruction may be a part of education, but education is far more than instruction. The less academically inclined the pupil, the more this is true. Instruction contributes to education only inasmuch as it is experienced and absorbed. Consequently it is necessary to devise learning situations in which the pupils can work out answers in their own way. (Paragraph 41)

A major contribution to educational retardation is social and intellectual deprivation. One of the more powerful antidotes is experience. Many of the successful experiments in secondary schools are looking for ways to help pupils digest the experience they already have and to offer them new experience which is felt to be relevant. They aim to start from a question the pupils consider interesting and to devise experiences which will suggest an answer. Almost all teachers with long commitment to teaching boys and girls of this age and level of ability will agree that for their pupils an idea or a fact or an answer will become neither real, nor interesting, nor likely to be remembered, if it is not linked at a fairly basic level with something they have 'experienced' in a more tangible sense than that in which more able children can 'experience' the written word or the spoken exposition. (Paragraph 42)

Learning is an individual process requiring active involvement. The solution of a problem is a personal discovery. Many of the problems encountered in the modern humanities do not have one solution; then the pupils can be encouraged to discuss several rival interpretations and learn that there may be more than one right answer to a question. The real value of experience based learning is that the pupils try to think things out for themselves so that they learn from their mistakes as well as from their successes. (Paragraph 45)

Bibliography

Environmental studies
J. E. Archer and T. H. Dalton *Fieldwork in Geography* Batsford 1968
R. Douch *Local History and the Teacher* Routledge and Kegan Paul 1967
F. G. Emmison *Archives and Local History* Methuen 1966
A. Hammersley, E. Jones and G. A. Perry *Approaches to Environmental Studies Series* Blandford 1968
R. F. Mackenzie *Escape from the Classroom* Collins 1965
W. G. Vinal *Nature Recreation* Dover Publications 1963

The educational use of museums
Molly Harrison *Changing Museums* Longmans 1967
T. L. Low *The Museum as a Social Instrument* American Association of Museums 1942
B. R. Winstanley *Children and Museums* Blackwell 1967
Museum School Services The Museums Association 1967
The Museum and the School Historical Association 1961

Museums, galleries and sites to visit
Ancient Monuments and Historic Buildings Open to the Public HMSO published annually
Country Houses Open to the Public Country Life 1963
Guide to National Museums and Galleries in London HMSO 1968
Historic Houses in Britain Index Publications published annually
Museums and Galleries in Great Britain Index Publications published annually
The National Trust Atlas Newnes and Index Publications 1966
The Shell Nature Lover's Atlas Michael Joseph and Ebury Press 1966

Books for children
M. Kirby *Meet me in Trafalgar Square* Schoolmaster 1968
A. White *Visiting Museums* Faber 1968

Useful addresses

Societies dealing with the arrangement of visits
British Holidays and Travel Association, 64 St James Street, London SW1.
Central Bureau for Visits and Exchanges, 55a Duke Street, London WIM 5DH.
School Journey Association, 23 Southampton Place, London WCI.
Youth Hostels Association, Trevelyan House, St Albans, Herts.

Societies interested in appreciation and conservation
The Civic Trust, 79 Buckingham Palace Road, London SW1.
The Council for Nature, 41 Queen's Gate, London SW7.
The Council of Industrial Design, 28 Haymarket, London SW1.
The Georgian Group, 2 Chester Street, London SW1.
The Housing Centre Trust, 13 Suffolk Street, London SW1.
The National Buildings Record, Fielden House, Great College Street, London SW1.
The Nature Conservancy, 19 Belgrave Square, London SW1.
The National Trust, 23 Caxton Street, London SW1.
The Rural Industries Bureau, 35 Camp Road, London SW19.
The Society for the Preservation of Rural England, 4 Hobart Place, London SW1.
The Society for the Protection of Ancient Buildings, 55 Great Ormond Street, London WCI.
The Victorian Society, 12 Magnolia Wharf, Strand-on-the-Green, London W4.

Index